A Stoic's Guide to Starting a Digital Business

Strategies and Wisdom

Table of Contents

Chapter 1. Introduction

Immerse yourself in the realm of both ancient wisdom and modern entrepreneurship with our Special Report: "A Stoic's Guide to Starting a Digital Business: Strategies and Wisdom". It's like nothing you've seen before, a harmonious blend of stoic philosophy and insightful strategies, tailored perfectly to guide you through the nuanced stages of launching your digital venture. It doesn't matter whether you are an aspiring entrepreneur or a seasoned businessperson wanting to explore digital horizons, this guide is filled to the brim with golden nuggets of practical advice and zen-like wisdom. What you'll find within isn't just a guide on starting a business, it's a life-changing blueprint for triumph against the odds, seamlessly aligning age-old Stoic principles with the exciting world of digital commerce. Engaging, inspiring, and remarkably elucidating, this Special Report is bound to pique your curiosity, ignite your passion, and set you on the path to becoming the digital entrepreneur that you're meant to be.

Chapter 2. The Stoic Foundation: Unraveling Philosophy for Entrepreneurs

Entrepreneurship, while frequently lauded for its innovative scope and potential for economic growth, is, at its core, an endeavor characterized by uncertainty and risk. It requires resilience, grit, and a certain unwavering determination that seems to teeter on the brink of stubbornness. Ironically, it is these very qualities that Stoicism, an ancient school of Hellenistic philosophy, seeks to instill in its practitioners. Stoicism, for the uninitiated, is a philosophy that encourages virtue, tolerance, and self-control, yielding resilience and calmness in the face of adversity.

2.1. Stoicism: A Brief Introduction

Stoicism takes its name from the location in which it was first taught: the Stoa Poikile or "painted porch", an open market in Athens. It was propagated by its early fathers like Epictetus, Seneca the Younger, and Emperor Marcus Aurelius, and it has its foundations in accepting the world as it is, not as we'd like it to be. Its pragmatic and realistically grounded approach to life makes it a fitting philosophy for entrepreneurs to study and apply to their business journeys.

In its essence, Stoicism asserts that we do not control and cannot rely on external events. Rather, we're respectively responsible for our own actions and reactions. This philosophy urges individuals to focus their energy on the aspects they can influence, thereby fostering a practical approach to life's challenges - a skill that is highly relevant in modern entrepreneurship.

2.2. Connecting Stoicism with Entrepreneurship

An entrepreneur's journey involves innumerable challenges. The Stoic approach of focusing on our own actions and responses can provide a sturdy foundation that can hold one steady in turbulent entrepreneurial waters.

In business, many factors like market conditions, competition behavior, and consumer preferences are uncontrollable. A Stoic entrepreneur takes this as an undeniable truth and diverts focus to areas where control can be exerted. This might involve refining the business model, seeking efficient resources, enhancing product or service quality, designing innovative marketing strategies, or improving customer service.

Applying Stoicism in entrepreneurship also implies not being swayed by successes or setbacks. Stoics believe that both success and failure are ephemeral and that rewarding or punishing oneself excessively for either could hamper the ultimate long-term goals. This ability to maintain level-headedness is crucial in the roller-coaster ride of starting a new venture where soaring highs and crashing lows are part of the journey.

2.3. Stoic Principles and their Entrepreneurial Applications

Following are some key Stoic principles that are worth exploring for their potential to guide and mold an enduring entrepreneur.

2.3.1. The Dichotomy of Control

This Stoicism principle is about dividing items into two categories: things you can control (such as your beliefs, judgments, desires, and actions) and things you can't control (including the past, nature, and the action of others).

As an entrepreneur, you will benefit from focusing your energy on what you can control. For instance, you can't control market volatility but you can design your business strategy to adapt to this volatility.

2.3.2. Virtuous Action

Stoics see virtue as the highest good and the main component of a fulfilling life. Virtue, in this sense, refers to excellence in character and involves qualities such as wisdom, courage, justice, and temperance.

In the context of entrepreneurship, this might translate into practicing ethical business, developing fair policies, maintaining transparency, and providing value-packed products or services to customers.

2.3.3. Maintain Objective Judgment

Stoics emphasize objective judgment, suggesting that things are not necessarily good or bad in themselves. Instead, our judgments make them appear so. They encourage us to perceive matters objectively and not judge them based on preconceived beliefs or biases.

In business, this might translate to being open-minded, embracing innovative ideas, and assessing market trends objectively to bring about necessary changes in your venture.

2.4. Practical Stoicism in Business

Strategies and principles are helpful only when applied. Therefore, as an entrepreneur, knowing Stoicism is only half the journey. Introducing Stoic practices into your everyday business strategies is an effective way of ingraining this philosophy into your entrepreneurial venture.

Focusing on your reactions and responses during a business crisis, not overdramatizing losses or underplaying victories, and practicing constant self-improvement and innovation with virtue in the driver's seat could be your first steps towards applying Stoicism in your entrepreneurial journey. Remember, Stoicism isn't about disowning emotions or being unaffected; it's about rational understanding of situations and controlling the controllable in the most efficient way possible.

In conclusion, Stoicism offers an illuminating lens through which to view and navigate the entrepreneurial journey. At its very core, Stoicism as a philosophy is potent, applicable, and timelessly beneficial, making it infinitely suitable for entrepreneurs grappling with the intricacies of the digital realm. From managing unforeseen crises to cultivating an enduring and resilient business model, Stoicism provides the foundation required to weather the intensities of the entrepreneurial journey. It fosters in entrepreneurs a deep appreciation for the power within themselves, further enhancing their abilities to navigate the unpredictable seas of entrepreneurship.

Chapter 3. Fostering the Mindset: Adopting Stoic Principles in Business

It all begins within the mind. Your external world is but a reflection of your internal thoughts and convictions. Understanding this simple yet profound principle is your first step towards success, not just in business but in any endeavor you undertake. Embracing stoic principles into your business venture affords you not just clarity in times of chaos but perseverance amidst uncertain scenarios as well. Stoic philosophy, dating back to the 3rd century BC, is a practical philosophy centered around focusing on what you control, accepting what you can't, and identifying the difference between these two. We will delve deeper into these ideas throughout this section.

3.1. Embrace Your Inner Entrepreneur

Being an entrepreneur is more than owning a company, more than setting up a shop online. It's about a mindset, a desire to create, an ambition to succeed, a thirst to learn, and the tenacity to survive failures. It's an ever-changing process, and as a stoic, you understand and accept this. You appreciate that your business venture is but a part of the bigger journey that is life itself, and setbacks are not failures, just rungs on the ladder to success.

This stoic approach helps foster your determination. Obstacles no longer look like insurmountable challenges, rather they appear as lessons. When problems arise, as they invariably would in your entrepreneurial journey, as a stoic, you're better equipped to handle them with calmness and composure, considering them to be a part of your journey rather than calamities. This mindset is crucial, setting one up for long-term success and sustainability in the uncertain realm of entrepreneurship.

3.2. Unleashing Your Stoic Potential

To truly understand the depth of stoicism, you must try to comprehend two significant principles: the Dichotomy of Control, and the Principle of Objectivity.

1. **Dichotomy of Control:**

According to the Stoic philosopher Epictetus, there are things in life that we have no control over and things that we do. Understanding this idea and applying it to your business can drastically change how you react to speed bumps along the way.

As you launch your digital venture, keep reminding yourself of what is within your control: your efforts, your dedication, the strategies you employ, and how you react to challenges that come your way. Conversely, know that there are many elements outside your control: the economy, market trends, consumer behavior, and global crises.

Accept this dichotomy with grace. This will ensure that your energy is spent on things that truly matter, saving you from unnecessary anxiety and heartache.

1. **The Principle of Objectivity:**

The stoic principle of objectivity encourages us to view situations as they are, not imbuing them with unnecessary emotions or biases. Training ourselves to apply this principle allows us to see challenges clearly, stripped of the fear and anticipation that often cloud our judgment and decision-making abilities.

When a problem arises, analyze it objectively, not as a catastrophe but as a scenario that demands your problem-solving skills. See it for what it is, rather than what it could mean for your business. This outlook will help you make calculated decisions, free of panic and haste.

3.3. The Unlearning Process

Adopting a stoic mindset for your business venture isn't just about learning these principles. It's equally about unlearning a lot of things that we've been conditioned to believe. In entrepreneurship, unlearning is just as critical as learning.

Stoic philosophy teaches us to question the status quo, to scrutinize our concept of success and failure, and to redefine them in ways that serve our purpose and our personal peace. This unlearning process can be challenging since it requires letting go of deeply ingrained beliefs. But when you do conquer it, the serenity and clarity you achieve will make the effort worthwhile.

3.4. Applying Stoicism in the Digital Age

The challenges of starting and running a digital business can be daunting. Competition can be fierce, trends change overnight, and consumer behavior can be unpredictable. In the face of such uncertainties, a stoic mindset can be your guiding light.

1. **Focusing on Actionable Metrics:**

One of the primary principles of stoicism is focusing on what you can control, and in digital business, one of these factors is your understanding of user behavior and trends through actionable metrics. Focus on analyzing data that actually impacts your business, and avoid getting drowned in vanity metrics.

1. **Embracing Change:**

Stoicism encourages acceptance of the inevitable, and change in a digital business landscape is one such element. Businesses that survive and thrive are the ones that understand and accept this fact. Being adaptable and willing to evolve your strategies in alignment with market changes can give you a competitive edge.

1. **Practicing Patience:**

The digital world can sometimes give an illusion of instant success. But a stoic understands that real growth takes time and patience.

Remember that adopting stoic principles in your business venture isn't about depriving yourself of emotions. It's about not allowing your emotions to cloud your judgment and actions. It's a grounding tool kit that fosters mindfulness, wisdom, and resilience. Armed with these stoic principles, you'll be better prepared not just to start a digital business, but to navigate the joys and challenges it brings along, to ultimately mold a venture that is not only profitable but also emotionally rewarding.

This brings to a close our dive into adopting stoic principles in business. While the journey may seem daunting, remember Marcus Aurelius's words: "The impediment to action advances action. What stands in the way becomes the way". In every obstacle lies an opportunity, if only you possess the stoic mindset to see and seize it.

Chapter 4. The Basics of Digital Business Strategies: A Stoic's Perspective

It goes without saying that the journey to a successful digital business often finds its roots in a well-crafted strategy. From the Stoic's point of view, strategy isn't something detached from the essence of life, but an integral part of it. As Seneca echoes through time, "Luck is what happens when preparation meets opportunity."

4.1. Embrace the Virtues of Resilience

Resilience, in this context, is about having the mental fortitude to endure the inevitable challenges and adversities that come with pioneering a new venture. A digital entrepreneur, like the Stoic, understands that volatility is an inherent aspect of the business landscape, and learns how to turn stumbling blocks into stepping stones.

An investment in a solid digital infrastructure will embody this resilience. The influx of disruptive technology – think artificial intelligence, machine learning and big data – makes it easy to deploy and scale digital solutions. A Stoic embraces this power of adaptability. By creating a system that can handle disruptions, you are putting into practice the Stoic resilience.

4.2. Understand Your Sphere of Control

The Stoic philosopher Epictetus made a profound distinction between things we can control and the things we cannot. To a Stoic, understanding this simple truth provides clarity in decision making and alleviates unnecessary stress.

This perspective is valuable in the world of digital business strategy. For example, you cannot dictate the market nor predict every customer's preference, but you can control your business model, the products/services you offer, and the customer experience you deliver. Focus your efforts on elements within your sphere of control. If something fails, instead of dwelling on what went wrong, think about how to adjust and move forward.

4.3. Utilize the Power of Objectivity

The same technology that enables our digital enterprises can also generate excessive noise that clouds our judgment. Here, the Stoic idea of objectivity, seeing things for what they really are, comes in handy.

Employ data analytics and other technological advances to your advantage. Use them not only as a means to assess your business's performance but also to uncover unseen trends across your industry. By being vigilant and by adapting based on this objective analysis, you can navigate through the fast-paced digital seas.

4.4. Keeping a Long-Term Perspective in Mind

Much like the wisdom of the Stoics, a good business strategy doesn't discount the future for present gains. It's always seeking a balance, taking into consideration the long-term sustainability of the business.

In terms of digital business, this could involve differentiating between fleeting trends and lasting changes. For instance, while the rise of a new social media platform may seem like a golden opportunity for marketing, jumping onto every new trend may distract from achieving your core business objectives. A Stoic keeps his eye on the prize, remaining unperturbed by the ebb and flow of technologies.

4.5. The Practice of Negative Visualization

It might seem counterintuitive, but Stoics find great utility in imagining the worst-case scenarios. This aids in removing the fear of the unknown and also helps them prepare for potential setbacks.

This technique can be applied to your digital business strategy. By routinely conducting risk assessments or threat modeling, you can anticipate potential issues, create contingency plans, and react swiftly and efficiently when faced with crises.

4.6. A Final Word

In this digital age, the competition is no longer with your rivals; it's against time, against the speed at which the world is changing. However, with the inherent philosophy of Stoicism acting as your lighthouse, you can navigate through turbulent waters.

Always remember, good business strategy, just like Stoic wisdom, isn't about predicting the future. It's about preparing for it.--

Chapter 5. Calm before the Storm: Risk Assessment and Mitigation

In the realm of digital entrepreneurship, nothing commences without first understanding and acknowledging the possibility of risks. Grasping and aligning with this tenet forms the base of stoic philosophy, teaching us that equanimity amidst chaos is a result of preparation and acceptance rather than good fortune. We are here to pilfer from past wisdom and apply it to the innovational world of digital commerce.

5.1. Prelude: The Stoic Vision of Risk

To start, we must understand that a stoic views risk differently than most. To them, risk is an inevitable part of life, and therefore, of business as well. Failures aren't deflections from the journey, but a part of it. The Stoics teach us to examine, accept and prepare for these risks. This approach, when adopted for business risk assessment and mitigation, can prove liberating and transformative.

5.2. Identifying Potential Risks

The first step is a clear evaluation of potential risks. Risk identification is a dynamic process and should be conducted frequently. It involves being proactive and objective in recognizing risk-factors that could plague your venture during its journey. For a digital business, these can range from technological shortcomings, operational challenges, market competition, to regulatory compliance issues.

```
[sources]
- Internal workshop analysis
- Market research
- Industry trends
- Interviews with customers
- Feedback from stakeholders
```

Each source offers valuable insights into potential risks that could arise. Confronting these risks from a stoic perspective involves accepting them as potential realities, not catastrophes to be feared.

5.3. Categorizing the Risks

Merely identifying risks isn't enough. They need to be categorized to help prioritize and plan next steps. All risks are not made equal; some require immediate attention while others may be dealt with at a later stage. Classifying based on their severity, probability, and potential impact can help sort them into an organized structure.

```
[severity] High, Medium, Low
[probability] Highly Likely, Likely, Unlikely
[impact] Severe, Moderate, Mild
```

By categorizing risks, we are effectively taming the chaotic nature of unforeseen circumstances, making them visible, understandable and manageable.

5.4. Analyzing the Risks

A stoic entrepreneur doesn't stop at identification or categorization. Stoicism extols us to delve deeply into understanding each risk - its direct and indirect implications, its potential reach and more. This process, known as risk analysis, can help connect the dots between different risk factors and reveal overarching themes that need to be addressed.

Involving all stakeholders in the analysis process can whittle out a wider perspective, thus enriching the outcomes of this exercise.

5.5. Risk Response Planning

Like a stoic warrior ready to embrace the battlefield, having understood and analyzed the enemy, the next step is to prepare a response. This is a crucial phase where action plans are formulated to mitigate, accept, or avoid the identified risks. Response planning also includes setting up contingency measures for risks that might still occur despite preventative measures.

Remember, stoicism teaches us to be prepared and adapt, not be passive. Therefore, developing robust response plans and being equipped to act decisively is key.

5.6. Implementing the Risk Mitigation Strategies

With ample preparation in place, it's time to implement these plans. This involves active monitoring, allocating resources, setting up communication channels, and ensuring that risk mitigation strategies are integrated into the day-to-day operations of your digital venture. Your mindset should be proactive rather than reactive.

5.7. Regular Risk Reviews

The digital business landscape is as dynamic as the philosophy of stoicism itself. As markets, technology, and customer behaviour fluctuate, so do associated risks. Regular risk review sessions should be a part of your business model to continually assess and retrofit your mitigation strategies in line with prevailing trends.

In conclusion, the stoic's approach to risk assessment and mitigation in digital entrepreneurship isn't just about mechanical steps. It's an integrated, evolving philosophy that empowers us to embrace adversity, learn from it, and transmute it into an opportunity. As we venture into the world of digital commerce, let's remember what Epictetus said, "We should always be asking ourselves: 'Is this something that is, or is not, in my control?'"

Chapter 6. Gearing Up: Business Planning with a Stoic Mindset

To the Stoics, the mind was a fortress. A place impenetrable by external circumstances, where reason alone dictated action. Building a business with a Stoic mindset is to armor ourselves against the trials and tribulations entrepreneurship invariably brings, channeling adversity into fueled ambition and unwavering resolve. We begin this chapter by introducing the primary facets of Stoicism and how they inform effective business planning.

6.1. Stoic Principles for Business Planning

The core values of Stoicism – wisdom, courage, justice, and temperance, perfectly align with the requirements of business planning, for they signify understanding, bravery, fairness, and restraint respectively. An entrepreneur who exercises these virtues is less likely to be swayed by emotions, focusing instead on rational decision-making. This fundamental alignment signifies finding balance in our actions: seeking truth, facing uncertainties, ensuring fairness, and exercising moderation in all we do.

For this, we must understand our business's purpose and align our plans and actions accordingly, ensuring our desires and decisions are coherently structured and free from distracting, unattainable aims. Such rational and disciplined approach gives life to long-term, sustainable success.

6.2. The Business Plan: A Stoic Framework

A business plan built on Stoic principles doesn't merely focus on profit margins and revenue forecasts. It veers deeper into understanding the dynamics of the industry, its own strengths and weaknesses, and ultimately, how it aligns with our life's purpose. To begin, we break down the components of a traditional business plan and illuminate how a Stoic might approach them.

Executive Summary: As the snapshot of your business, this section should clearly outline your objectives and give the reader a brief introduction of what the business does. Here, align the vision for the business with your personal purpose and the Stoic principles.

Company Description: Herein, detail your legal structure, location, and a bit about your product or service. Follow temperance by highlighting the essential aspects and avoid exaggerating the competencies.

Market Analysis: This section must be crafted with wisdom, as it carries the weight of understanding the trends, customer segments, and competition. React rationally to these insights instead of letting fear or ambition sway.

Organization and Management: Principle of justice should be at the forefront when designing the management structure and team formation. Everyone should be given their due role and responsibility, keeping fairness at the center of it all.

Services or Products: Detail what you're trading, how it benefits customers, and its life cycle. Here, courage takes center stage – have faith in your product and believe in its potential to succeed, despite hurdles along the way.

Marketing and Sales: Create a sales strategy which portrays the authentic value of your product to the potential customers avoiding deceit or falsehood. Remember, stoics believe in honesty and transparency.

Funding Request: Based on temperance, request only what is necessary for sustenance of the business without succumbing to the lure of excess.

Financial Projections: Apply wisdom and offer realistic predictions than overstating the profits or underplaying the costs. Let these numbers reflect your prudent understanding of the business environment.

6.3. Embracing Change: A Stoic's Ally

Epictetus, a renowned Stoic philosopher, famously said, "It's not what happens to you, but how you react to it that matters." In business, unforeseen changes are inevitable. Market dynamics shift, customer tastes evolve, technology advances - a business plan is not a monolith but a dynamic outline that must embrace change. A Stoic entrepreneur is flexible, adapting to new arenas, without perturbations of mind.

6.4. Stoic Mindset and Risk Assessment

Assessing potential risks involves identifying potential issues that could negatively impact your business and developing ways to mitigate them. Here, a Stoic entrepreneur practices negative visualization - contemplating on worst-case scenarios. This proactive approach aids in making balanced decisions, lessening the propensity for shocks.

6.5. Reflection and Learning: A Stoic's Lifelong Endeavour

The Stoic entrepreneur's journey doesn't end once the business plan is complete. Stoicism preaches lifetime learning - a commitment to continuously improve, learn from mistakes and apply new insights. Regularly reviewing and updating your business plan is an essential part of this learning.

To summarize, planning a business with a Stoic mindset is less about creating static documents, but cultivating a resilient mindset that can weather the storms of entrepreneurial life. It's about having a clear vision, tempered with wisdom and a thirst for growth. A Stoic entrepreneur embraces change, sees failure as just another lesson to be learned, and builds a business that not just survives, but thrives.

Chapter 7. Surviving the Digital Marketplace: Stoic Tools and Techniques

If you're embarking on a journey into the world of digital entrepreneurship, you must arm yourself with more than just technical skills and business acumen. As you navigate this digital marketplace's complexities, the Stoic philosophy's wisdom can be your guiding light. Stoic teachings of resilience, value-based decision making, and focusing on what's within our control can prove invaluable at every stage of your entrepreneurial journey.

7.1. The Digital Marketplace: Unpredictable Tides

The digital marketplace is a vast and volatile arena. New technologies continuously transform the landscape, and consumer behavior is constantly in flux. Against these forces, even the most carefully laid plans can be swept aside. Much like the Stoics faced the unpredictability of life, we face a similarly unpredictable business environment. But, as Stoics, we understand that resilience is the secret to survival. We can't control the tides, but we can learn to surf.

Marcus Aurelius, the Roman emperor and Stoic philosopher, wrote, "You have power over your mind – not outside events. Realize this, and you will find strength." Aurelius advocates for a robust internal locus of control. The marketplace will twist and turn, but we must remain imperturbable, steadfastly clinging to our values and vision.

7.2. Applying Stoic Resilience in the Digital Age

Stoicism stresses the importance of resilience—the ability to bounce back from setbacks and maintain equanimity amidst change. As an entrepreneur, you're going to encounter failures, criticism, and unforeseen challenges. Embrace these as opportunities for growth and learning rather than viewing them as insurmountable obstacles.

Apply this principle by adopting a growth mindset. Reframe challenges as opportunities for learning and treat failure as a stepping-stone towards success. Keep your focus on what you're learning instead of dwelling on what's going wrong. Resilience is an invaluable asset that will help you navigate the rough seas of entrepreneurship.

7.3. Value-Based Decision Making: The Stoic Way

Just like in life, business decisions can have far-reaching consequences. In Stoic philosophy, the only good things are virtues such as wisdom, justice, courage, and moderation, and the only evils are vices—the absence or opposites of these virtues.

When you run your business guided by Stoic principles, your decisions are shaped by your values rather than transient goals or immediate profit. Your business's value-driven core can make it stand out in the digital marketplace and breed loyalty among consumers who share similar values.

For instance, if justice is a virtue you uphold, ensure fairness in your business dealings—be it in pricing your products, dealing with vendors, or treating your employees. If courage is your virtue, dare to innovate and stray off the beaten path. In an oversaturated digital marketplace, this courage will help your business stand out.

Reflect, then, not just on the immediate payoff of a business decision, but also whether it aligns with your core values. This long-term approach may lead to slower growth, but it will build a resilient, sustainable, and loved brand.

7.4. The Dichotomy of Control: A Stoic Solution for Entrepreneurial Anxiety

Entrepreneurship comes with a considerable amount of uncertainty and stress, which can lead to decision fatigue, burnout, and paralysis in the face of tough decisions. Here Stoic ideas can be a panacea—the dichotomy of control.

Stoics distinguish between things we can control (our beliefs, judgments, actions) and things we can't (receptions, outcomes). By focusing on our efforts instead of outcomes, we can reduce anxiety and work with clear minds.

In the context of a digital business, varied elements lie outside of your control—market trends, competitors, consumer behavior. You cannot control whether a customer will buy your product, whether a competitor will launch a similar product or whether a market crash will happen. Diverting your mental energy and efforts in this direction is futile and breeds anxiety.

So, direct your energy and resources towards your product quality, marketing efforts, customer service - factors that are within your control. Here you have the power to effect change and consequently influence, albeit indirectly, the elements outside of your control.

7.5. Embracing the View from Above: A Stoic Perspective on Business Success and Failure

Lastly, remember that Stoicism encourages a 'view from above'— it urges us to consider our lives and roles from a wider perspective to understand their transience and insignificance in the grand scheme of things. Apply this to both the highs and lows of your business journey. Every victory and every defeat is temporary and inconsequential in the universe's vast expanse.

Entrepreneurial success or failure does not define your worth. Celebrate your victories, learn from your failures, but never lose sight of your values and virtues that truly shape who you are.

The Stoic entrepreneurs, then, are more than just business owners—they are resilient surfers of the digital tide, philosophers with laptops, governed by virtues, propelled by their locus of control, and empowered by a cosmic perspective. Keep these Stoic tools and techniques in your entrepreneurial arsenal as you brave the unpredictable, thrilling venture that is digital entrepreneurship.

Chapter 8. Growing amidst Chaos: Stoic Strategies for Business Expansion

8.1. Understanding Chaos in Business

Success in the world of business is rarely a straight, predictable path. When navigating the highs and lows, it is common to encounter chaos or uncertainty. The stoic philosophers of ancient Greece and Rome understood deeply that life is filled with uncertainty. They advocated embracing, rather than fearing, the inevitable turbulence that life throws our way. Their wisdom is timeless and applies as much to today's fast-paced business world as it did to the rocky terrain of ancient life.

The first thing to understand about chaos is that it's not always an external force. It's not just about economic downturns, fierce competitors, or regulatory issues. Chaos can also come from within; lack of a clear strategy, dysfunctional teams, or lacking a clear understanding of your customers. It's crucial to diagnose the kind of chaos you face before you can harness it for your advantage.

8.2. Finding Calm within the Chaos

A key tenet of stoicism is that we do not have control over everything that happens to us. We only have control over how we react to it. This perspective is both liberating and empowering as it puts you in the driver's seat, regardless of what's swirling around.

When it comes to your business, always remember that the 'market shapes the business', and not the other way around. If you try to bend the chaos to your will rather than riding its wave, you risk crashing rather than soaring.

The stoic approach to finding calm in chaos lies in recognizing where your control lies - in your responses, actions, and attitude. Embrace the concept of amor fati, a stoic notion that translates to 'love of one's fate'. Rather than wasting energy regretting or battling the unpredictable, honor it as an essential part of your business journey.

8.3. Building Resilience

Stoicism encourages individuals to prepare for adversity, building resilience both personally and professionally. This concept applies seamlessly to business expansion. The bigger you grow, the more challenges you are likely to face. Hence, a resilient mindset is crucial.

Relinquishing attachment to specific outcomes and focusing instead on your responses can help you build a formidable business capable of weathering any storm. Resilience in a business context isn't just about durability; it's about flexibility, adaptiveness, and the ability to convert adversity into opportunity.

8.4. Expanding Without Losing Your Balance

When plotting a course for business expansion, it's easy to get swept up in the excitement and ambition. Stoicism warns against such unbridled enthusiasm without careful consideration. Any move towards growth needs to be balanced with a stoic self-reflection.

Marcus Aurelius, a well-known stoic philosopher, advises us to always ask, "Is this necessary?" Applying this to our business decisions forces us to scrutinize our plans and separate mere wants from genuine needs. Our resources, as endless as they may seem, are finite, and every course of action taken consumes some of these resources. By maintaining a balanced approach, you ensure that your business expansion won't compromise the integrity of your core operation.

8.5. Forged in Adversity: Leveraging Difficult Times for Growth

In the sage words of Seneca, another noted stoic philosopher, "Difficulties strengthen the mind, as labor does the body." By repositioning obstacles as opportunities for growth, every challenge you come across becomes a stepping-stone to further expansion.

Every setback, shortcoming, or hurdle that your business faces is not a drawback but is a chance to recalibrate, learn, and inch closer towards your goal. This shift in perspective turns any business owner, manager, or employee into a stoic entrepreneur equipped with the wisdom to navigate any turbulence.

8.6. Conclusion

In the volatile realm of business, nothing is guaranteed except change. Growth can either be a daunting venture or an exciting journey, depending on how you perceive and react to it. By adopting stoic strategies, staying resilient and mindful, and perceiving uncertainties as opportunities rather than setbacks, business owners can navigate the path of expansion with grace and confidence.

Remember, your business, like all of life's ventures, grows amidst chaos, not despite it. In the wise words of Marcus Aurelius, "The impediment to action advances action. What stands in the way becomes the way." Embrace the stoic way and watch your business thrive amidst the seeming chaos.

Chapter 9. Riding the Waves: Embracing Change and Adversity

As an initiate to the realm of digital entrepreneurship, it's inevitable to encounter both change and adversity. These are the waves that contour the landscape of business, yielding opportunities for those colossal enough to ride them. However, the skill of riding these waves isn't an inherent talent we are born with. It must be honed with both wisdom and experience.

In the words of the ancient Stoic philosopher Epictetus, "It's not what happens to you but how you react to it that matters." As with the waves of the sea, change and adversity in business can either crash and upend you, or you can hone your surf skills, and utilize their power to propel your business forward. This chapter is a detailed guide in developing the mindset and skills required to turn obstacles into opportunities.

9.1. Harnessing the Power of Change

Change is akin to the seasons—spring, summer, autumn, winter — each brings a transformation with it. The same applies to the business ecosystem. New technologies blossom, trends shift, customer expectations evolve, and economic conditions fluctuate. A successful digital entrepreneur embraces these changes, confident in their ability to adapt.

In our modern digitized world, change often comes from technological innovation. Every advancement provides novel opportunities for value creation. It could be a new software to streamline processes, a new platform to reach potential customers, or an entirely new technology that could disrupt your industry.

There's an adage in the world of entrepreneurship: Innovate or die. As cold as it may seem, it communicates an uncomfortable truth. Standing still in the face of change won't lead to success. You need to move, and more importantly, pivot in the right direction.

Learning to navigate change successfully requires both a tactical and strategic mindset. Tactically, a digital entrepreneur must stay attuned to industry trends and technological advancements. They should frequently invest time to research, attend industry-related seminars and training, and network with others in their industry.

Strategically, entrepreneurs must build flexibility into their business models. This involves creating contingency plans, diversifying revenue streams, and fostering a growth mindset among the team. Remember the Stoic principle of focusing your energy on what you can control - your actions and responses.

9.2. Confronting Adversity

If change in business is inevitable, adversity is its enigmatic twin. It looms both expectedly and unexpectedly, a threatening wave building before an entrepreneur's voyage. Yet, as a Stoic entrepreneur, one does not shirk from its sight, rather takes it as an occasion to demonstrate resilience.

Marcus Aurelius, a well-known Stoic and a Roman Emperor, remarked, "The impediment to action advances action. What stands in the way becomes the way." This is the heart of the entrepreneur's approach to adversity - seeing it not as a dead-end, but the path forward.

Adversity manifests in various forms – unforeseen expenses, disgruntled customers, product failures, or even personal life crises. Stoic philosophy encourages us to view these adversities objectively. Instead of resigning to misfortune, ask yourself: "What can I learn from this situation? What can I improve upon moving forward?"

In any hard situation, remind yourself to separate the facts of the situations from the implied negative emotions. This objective thinking is the core skill of resilience and can immensely reduce the impact adversity has on you.

Building resilience isn't one-time armor that shields you from all future adversity; it's part and parcel of an ongoing journey, much like honing a muscle. Reading and reflecting on Stoic writings, meditating, seeking mentorship, and expressing gratitude are all ways an entrepreneur can enhance their resilience.

9.3. Charting the Course: A Practical Toolkit

Now that we've examined how to harness change and confront adversity through a stoic lens, let's tackle actionable steps an entrepreneur can take to implement these principles.

1. Maintain a Weekly Change Log: Write down all significant changes you notice in your business or industry every week. At least once a month, review these logs and brainstorm how you can adapt to or leverage these changes.

2. Develop a Contingency Plan: Identify key risks in your business and develop contingency plans for each. This will not only provide you clarity during crises, but also offer a sense of control which significantly reduces stress.

3. Practice Resilience Building: Develop habits that build resilience. This could range from daily meditation, reading Stoic philosophy, maintaining a gratitude journal, or cultivating a hobby outside your business to maintain a balanced perspective.

4. Create a Learning Plan: Keep up with the newest trends and technologies relevant to your industry. This could involve subscribing to industry publications, attending trade shows or webinars, networking with industry peers, or even joining a

mastermind group.

By approaching your entrepreneurial journey with an open mind, adaptable spirit, and fortified resilience, you're not only capable of riding the waves of change and adversity but are also poised to leverage them as vehicles towards growth. With Stoic wisdom as your compass, you are well-equipped to transform every challenge into an opportunity for both personal and business evolution.

Chapter 10. Sustaining Success: Applying Stoicism in Long-term Business Operations

Once a business reaches a certain level of success, our instinct is often to relax and enjoy the fruits of our labour. We might even believe we've won; that the war has been fought and we've emerged victorious. But in reality, the pinnacle of success marks a new phase of your journey—the phase of sustaining success. According to the ancient Stoics, our characters are tested not in moments of adversity, but when we taste success. The true challenge lies in not getting complacent but being ever ready to maintain this hard-earned success.

10.1. Stoicism and Sustaining Success

The principles of Stoic philosophy offer a potent toolkit for maintaining long-term business success. These principles remind us not to be swept away by temporary victories but to continue striving for sustained success by fostering humility, resilience, and integrity.

Stoicism teaches us to focus on elements within our control, accept those that are not, and discern between the two. This wisdom is crucial to successful, ongoing operations of your digital business. We have little control over market trends, user behavior, or competition, but we can control our reactions to these circumstances, our business strategies, and ethical standards. By maintaining focus on what you can control, you minimize business menace, ensuring consistent progress towards your goals.

10.2. Humility and the Path to Enlightened Leadership

A key tenet of Stoicism is humility. At the heart of sustaining long-term successes is an equally long-term leader—one who embodies Stoic humility. Humility prevents pride and arrogance from distorting judgments and decisions, ensuring your continued openness to new ideas, technologies, and strategies crucial in the rapidly evolving digital world.

Maintain your humility by consciously recognizing the efforts of those who have contributed to your success, including your employees, customers, and business partners. Acknowledge that your success is a result of various factors, many outside your personal efforts. Such perspective keeps you grounded and protects you from impulsive, ego-driven decisions.

10.3. Resilience in Times of Calm and Storm

Stoicism's emphasis on resilience has significant implications for the inevitable ebb and flow of your business's journey. By building mental fortitude in good times, you prepare yourself for potential downturns. Stoics believe that hardships are opportunities for growth and learning, which are vital for long-term business operations.

The digital landscape is by nature volatile, ever-changing, and unpredictable. Building resilience helps you view these sudden changes not as threats, but as opportunities—opportunities to learn, adapt, and grow. Resilient individuals twist adversity into advantage, making effective resilience strategies non-negotiable in your arduous journey towards sustained success.

10.4. Building Business Integrity

This stoic inspired approach to leadership also champions the cultivation of virtue for its own sake. In terms of your business operations, this translates into upholding the highest standards of integrity throughout your organization.

Business integrity inspires trust among your stakeholders, including customers, employees, and investors, which is fundamental for your business's long-term viability. The presence of trust can create a powerful brand, loyal customer base, and dedicated workforce, ultimately leading to continued growth and sustainable success.

10.5. Adapting to Change

Stoicism instructs us to embrace change as a natural order of life. Similarly, digital businesses require constant adaptation. Technology evolves, market demands shift, and competition grows fiercer. By staying flexible and open to change, you are better equipped to pivot your efforts to match current market trends and stay ahead of your competition.

Embracing change also encourages innovation in your organization by fostering a culture that values new ideas and continuous learning. By viewing change not just as a natural occurrence but as an impetus for innovation, businesses can use the transience of the digital world to their benefit.

10.6. Implementation of Stoicism in Daily Business

How does one effectively implement these principles of Stoicism in daily business operations? It is all about practice. Regular reflection on both successes and failures can help instill these values deeply in your business culture.

With concerted effort, humility can be intrinsic in leadership styles; resilience can be tie-in with problem-solving methods; integrity can become the cornerstone of your company's reputation; and adaptability towards change can subsume every operational strategy.

Successfully sustaining a digital business is not a destination, but a continuous journey. By applying Stoic principles, you can make this journey richer, more balanced, and ultimately more successful. Embrace Stoicism not just as a philosophy, but as a lifestyle, and watch your digital enterprise flourish in the long term.

In conclusion, sustainably operating a digital business demands much more than financial acumen and innovative strategies; it requires a mindset that embraces change, values integrity, fosters resilience, and champions humility. By imbibing the ancient wisdom of Stoicism, digital entrepreneurs can navigate the complexities of today's digital landscape to build a profitable, sustainable, and ethical business.

Chapter 11. Reflection and Beyond: Continuous Improvement, the Stoic Way

As we make our way down this road of digital entrepreneurship, it's vital to understand that the refinement of our venture is a perpetual action. There are always new tools to implement, strategies to assess, or ideas to experiment with. And here's where Stoicism adds value – by fostering a reflective mindset that encourages continuous improvement in a balanced and sustainable way.

11.1. The Concept of Reflective Improvement

Reflective improvement entails a foreseeable cycle of retaining what works, discarding what doesn't, and relentlessly iterating. The Stoic perspective introduces an added layer, one that integrates reflection with emotional balance, focusing on what's within our control and accepting what's not.

According to Stoic philosophy, we should treat every experience as a lesson to learn something valuable and then use this knowledge to improve. This ability to self-reflect is what separates humans from all other beings, and harnessing it wisely is vital to personal growth and business excellence.

Related to a digital venture, your journey will overflow with moments stepping forth as lessons disguised as successes, failures, feedback, or trends – all waiting to be examined under the lens of your reflection.

11.2. Embracing Change: A Stoic Perspective

As the Greek stoic philosopher Heraclitus pointed out, "The only constant in life is change." In the modern digital landscape, this wisdom aligns perfectly. Today, technology evolves at an unprecedented pace, and the business that fails to adapt is often left behind.

As a stoic digital entrepreneur, embrace change as an essential part of the journey. Rather than resisting shifts in the market, consumer behaviour, or technological advancements, welcome them. They provide fertile ground for your venture to evolve, adapt, and strengthen itself over time.

11.3. The Virtue of Acceptance

However, recognizing that change is inevitable doesn't mean we can control every aspect of it. Stoicism teaches us to differentiate between what we can change and what we must accept. Distinguishing between the two shields us from the pointless stress of fighting unwinnable battles and allows us to focus our energy on areas where we can create a real impact.

In the context of a digital enterprise, certain elements will be outside your control. Market conditions, competitors' actions, or changing user behaviour are examples. Instead of wasting time and resources trying to alter these factors, a stoic entrepreneur redirects efforts into enhancing the business's controllable aspects - refining the product or service, improving user experience, or fortifying the brand.

11.4. The Value of Not Being Complacent

Complacency is the foe of progress, a quagmire trapping many businesses into a state of stagnation. As a stoic digital entrepreneur, it's incumbent on you to diligently guard against this. Find satisfaction in your achievements, indeed, but never allow that satisfaction to hinder your drive for continued improvement. Every accomplishment should serve as a stepping-stone toward something bigger, better, and more impactful.

11.5. Integrating Feedback: A Stoic Strategy

Stoicism can also teach us how to manage feedback constructively. Marcus Aurelius, the Roman Emperor and one of the most venerated Stoic philosophers, contended that inaccurate feedback is inconsequential and accurate feedback should be viewed not as criticism but an opportunity to learn and pivot. If someone points out an area where your digital venture could be improved, embrace it with gratitude, not resentment.

11.6. Cultivating Resilience

Resilience is woven into the fabric of Stoic philosophy and is particularly crucial in the digital entrepreneurship realm. The path to business success is seldom linear. There'll be setbacks and disappointments on this journey, but your ability to bounce back from them is a defining factor in your overall success. The manifestation of stoic resilience isn't just about recovery, but about emerging stronger, learning from the situation, and applying that wisdom to future challenges.

11.7. Conclusion: Stoicism and Continuous Improvement

Stoicism and continuous improvement share a common purpose: to advance, driven by wisdom gained from reflection, iteration, and resilience. When fused into your digital business strategy, they create an entrepreneurial philosophy both grounding and empowering.

Ultimately, the Stoic guidance to focus on what's within your control, accept what's not, embrace change, avoid complacency, and cultivate resilience, forms a potent strategy for an aspiring digital entrepreneur. This approach is more than just about commercial success; it's about creating a venture that is vibrant, adaptable, and sustainable. It's about shaping the future our digital world needs and deserves.